CHRISTMAS JAZZIN' ABOUT

PIANO/KEYBOARD

PAM WEDGWOOD

	page	CD track †		
Holly	1	**1**	2	3
Have Yourself a Merry Little Christmas	2	**4**	5	6
Good King Wenceslas	4	**7**	8	9
Christmas Jingle	6	**10**	11	12
Mary's Boy Child	8	**13**	14	15
On Christmas Night – I Saw Three Ships	10	**16**	17	18
Rudolph the Red-Nosed Reindeer	12	**19**	20	21
Silent Night	14	**22**	23	24
Sleigh Ride (Duet)	16	**25**	26	27
Santa Claus Is Comin' To Town (Duet)	20	**28**	29	30
O Come All Ye Swingin' Faithful (Duet)	26	**31**	32	33

† There are three CD tracks for each piece: a complete performance,
a backing track, and the backing track at a slower tempo.
A count-in of two bars is given before all the tracks.

FABER ƒƒ MUSIC

All other titles © 1994 by Faber Music Ltd
First published in 1994 by Faber Music Ltd
Bloomsbury House 74–77 Great Russell Street London WC1B 3DA
Music engraved by Wessex Music Services
Cover by Velladesign
Printed in England by Caligraving Ltd

ISBN10: 0-571-53404-X
EAN13: 978-0-571-53404-3

To buy Faber Music publications or to find out about the full range of titles available
please contact your local music retailer or Faber Music sales enquiries:

Faber Music Limited, Burnt Mill, Elizabeth Way, Harlow, CM20 2HX England
Tel: +44 (0)1279 82 89 82   Fax: +44 (0)1279 82 89 83
sales@fabermusic.com   fabermusic.com

1. Holly

2

2. Have Yourself a Merry Little Christmas

words and music by
Hugh Martin – Ralph Blane

3. Good King Wenceslas

With humour: Deep, crisp and evenly (♩. = 120)

6

4. Christmas Jingle

5. Mary's Boy Child

6. On Christmas Night – I Saw Three Ships

12

7. Rudolph the Red–Nosed Reindeer

© 1949 St Nicholas Music Inc. USA. Renewed 1977.
Warner Chappell Music Ltd, London W1Y 3FA.
This arrangement © 1994 St Nicholas Music Inc.

14

8. Silent Night

Slowly (♪ = 96)

Faster, with a lazy feel (♩. = 76)

15

9. Sleigh Ride (Duet)

Secondo

On a melody by Leroy Anderson

9. Sleigh Ride (Duet)

Primo

On a melody by Leroy Anderson

10. Santa Claus Is Coming To Town (Duet)

Secondo

10. Santa Claus Is Coming To Town (Duet)

Primo

11. O Come All Ye Swingin' Faithful (Duet)

Secondo

11. O Come All Ye Swingin' Faithful (Duet)

Primo